Cool Crafts

Sleepover Secrets

Stephanie Turnbull

A⁺
Smart Apple Media

Published by Smart Apple Media, an imprint of Black Rabbit Books
P.O. Box 3263, Mankato, Minnesota, 56002
www.blackrabbitbooks.com

Printed in the United States of America, at Corporate Graphics
in North Mankato, Minnesota

Designed and illustrated by Guy Callaby
Edited by Mary-Jane Wilkins

Cataloging-in-Publication Data is available from
the Library of Congress

ISBN 978-1-62588-378-0

Photo acknowledgements
t = top, bottom, c = center, l = left, r = right
page 1t Yobro10/Thinkstock, c xstockerx/Shutterstock; 2 Rafinade/
Thinkstock; 4t and subsequent pages Jan Mika; 5tl Africa Studio,
tr oksana2010, r tetyana radchenko, bl neiromobile, br and
subsequent Perfect Planning boxes Garsya, b Africa Studio;
6 Iuliia Azarova; 7 Jo Ann Snover; 8 Huntstock.com; 10b GVictoria;
12 shooarts; 13 Maridav; 14t Eldad Carin/all Shutterstock;
15c Mim Waller, b keki; 16 Sergey Goruppa; 17b OZaiachin;
18 Africa Studio; 19 Lena Ivanova; 20 Dragon Images;
21 Africa Studio; 22 tratong; 23 clarkfang/all Shutterstock
Cover clockwise from left MKucova, bennyartist, stanfram,
sunstock/all Thinkstock
Cover clockwise from bottom left sunstock, MKucova,
Yobro10, stanfram/all Thinkstock

DAD0061
022015
9 8 7 6 5 4 3 2 1

Contents

Time for fun!

Sleepovers are a fab way of having fun with friends, whether there are just two of you or a huge gang. The secret to great sleepovers is to plan activities everyone enjoys. Follow the tips in this book and you'll never be bored again!

Think crafty

Craft projects will keep you busy while you chat or listen to music. How about making jewelry or **origami** hearts? Or why not try sewing, knitting, and **weaving**?

Make sure you have basic supplies such as pens, paper, card, and scissors.

Be organized

Ask friends what they'd like to make and pick a project you'll all enjoy. Collect your craft supplies and make sure you have space to spread them out. Messy projects are better done at a kitchen table —don't end up with paint on the carpet or felt pen on your sofa!

Perfect Planning

Tidy up to make room for friends to spread out. Set out cushions or bean bags so everyone can relax while they get crafting.

Wear an apron or old clothes for messy crafts— and store supplies carefully!

Brilliant beads

Beads are perfect for colorful necklaces or bracelets. Collect as many as you can, give everyone lengths of string, ribbon, or thin elastic, and start threading.

Paper beads

To be a little more creative, why not make your own beads from gift wrap? It's easy to do and looks amazing.

1 in (2½ cm)

↔

↕

10 in (25 cm)

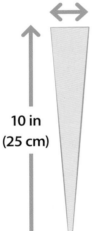

1. Draw a triangular shape on cardboard and cut it out. This is your template.

2. Draw around the template lots of times on a sheet of gift wrap. Cut out the triangles.

3. Starting at the wide end, roll a triangle around a thin paintbrush. Keep it straight. Cover the last bit with glue so it sticks down as you roll.

4. Gently slide the bead off the paintbrush. Make more, leave them to dry, then neaten the ends with sharp scissors.

5. Paint the beads with clear nail varnish to make them strong and shiny. Prop them up to dry.

Perfect Planning

Collect scraps of different gift wrap to see which colors and patterns work best.

6. Thread the beads on thin elastic. Add small plastic beads if you want.

Neat knotting

To make stylish bracelets and necklaces, knot string or cord to make a twisted braid. This clever knotting skill is called macramé.

1. *Find a ball of ordinary string and a few beads to thread on it. Cut two pieces of string, each about 6 feet 6 inches (2 m) long, and fold them in half.*

2. *Put the two strings together and tie a small loop in the top.*

The loop should be about the size of your biggest bead.

3. *Spread the strings on the table and trim the two middle ones to about half the length.*

4. *Now tie your first knot. Loop the left string over the two middle strings and behind the right string.*

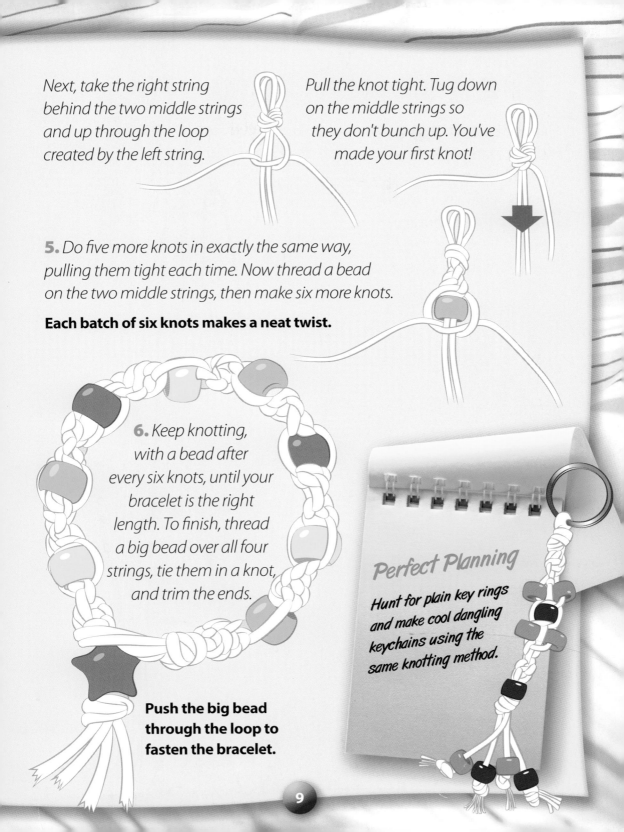

Next, take the right string behind the two middle strings and up through the loop created by the left string.

Pull the knot tight. Tug down on the middle strings so they don't bunch up. You've made your first knot!

5. Do five more knots in exactly the same way, pulling them tight each time. Now thread a bead on the two middle strings, then make six more knots.

Each batch of six knots makes a neat twist.

6. Keep knotting, with a bead after every six knots, until your bracelet is the right length. To finish, thread a big bead over all four strings, tie them in a knot, and trim the ends.

Push the big bead through the loop to fasten the bracelet.

Perfect Planning

Hunt for plain key rings and make cool dangling keychains using the same knotting method.

French knitting

French knitting uses a **spool** to make a long, thick cord of yarn. It's a skill that's easy to learn and fun to do in a group.

Making spools

Before friends arrive, make them each a spool.

1. *Find a thick cardboard tube and cut it into sections, each roughly 3 inches (8 cm) long.*

3 in (8 cm)

2. *Unfold four large paper clips.*

3. *Tape the clips around the tube. Bend each end out slightly.*

Perfect Planning

Why not personalize each friend's spool with their name and stickers?

Up-and-over knitting

Now you each need a ball of yarn and a big, fat needle.

1. Feed the yarn through the spool until 4 inches (10 cm) dangles beneath. Wrap the yarn around the back of a clip.

2. Wrap the yarn around the back of the next clip...

... and the next two, then back to the first. Keep the yarn above the first loop.

3. Hold the yarn tight with your left hand and use the needle to pull the lower loop up and over the clip. This is a stitch!

If you're left-handed, hold the yarn in your right hand.

4. Now wrap the yarn around the back of the next clip and pull the lower loop up and over, then move on to the next, and so on. A long snake of knitting will grow.

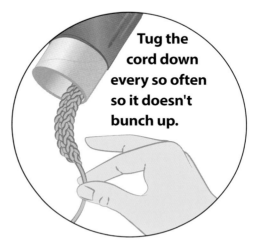

Tug the cord down every so often so it doesn't bunch up.

5. To finish, cut the yarn, leaving a long end. Take each loop off its clip and thread the cut end through. Pull tight.

6. Now use a new length of yarn to stitch the cord into a shape, for example a coiled rose.

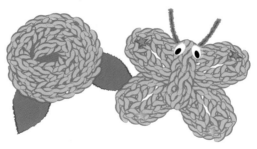

You can also weave yarn into strips. These make excellent bookmarks or cute scarves for soft toys!

Making a loom
First, you each need a frame called a **loom**.

1. Find four drinking straws and thread yarn through each.

Use lots of different colors to make bright stripes.

2. Tie the pieces of yarn together at the top and push the straws up to the knot. Stick **masking tape** around the top of the straws.

Start weaving

1. Tie the end of a ball of yarn around the first straw, pass the yarn under the second straw, over the third, and under the fourth.

2. Now go back over the fourth straw, under the third, over the second, and under the first. Weave more rows in the same way. Keep the yarn tight.

Push up the yarn as you go, so the rows are close together.

3. To finish a color, tie the yarn around an outside straw and cut the end. Start a new color as in step 1, tucking loose ends inside the weaving.

Perfect Planning

Buy a pack of colored straws and use the rest for slurping milkshakes while you weave!

4. When you reach the end, tie the yarn to an outer straw and cut it. Take off the tape and pull out the straws.

5. Push the weaving up to the top knot, tie another at the bottom and trim the loose ends.

Simple sewing

Sewing is a cool craft to do in a group. Use colorful felt—it's soft, easy to cut and doesn't fray at the edges.

Cute cookies

Start by making these easy felt cookies. You'll have a plateful in no time!

1. Draw around a cookie cutter on brown felt and cut out the shape. Make a smaller circle of white felt.

3. Find a few beads to look like sprinkles or cherries. Thread the needle with a matching color and tie both ends in a knot so that the thread is double.

Make sure the needle isn't too fat to go through the beads.

2. Thread a needle with white thread and tie a knot at the end. Sew the circles together with small stitches, going in and out of both layers. Knot the thread on the back and cut off any extra.

4. Sew on the beads. Don't forget to tie a knot at the back afterward.

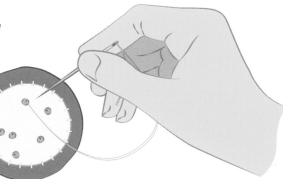

5. *Cut another brown circle and sew it to the first. When you're nearly all the way around, push in some cotton balls as stuffing, then sew the last bit.*

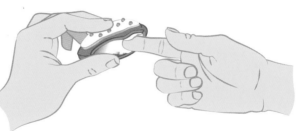

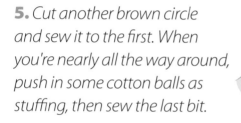

Make lots of cookies using different colors and toppings. Try sewing on loops of ribbon to hang them up, or attach them to bags or cushions with safety pins.

Perfect Planning

Hunt out special cookie cutters to make hanging decorations for Christmas and other celebrations.

Salt-dough sculpting

Why not get creative with a batch of home-made salt dough? Shape jewelry, figurines, name plates, or pencil pots.

Making dough

You need:
5 oz (150 g) flour
5 oz (150 g) salt
4 oz (130 ml) warm water
1 teaspoon vegetable oil

1. *Stir all the ingredients in a large bowl.*

2. *Make the mixture into a ball with your hands.* **Knead** *it on a floury surface for five minutes until it feels smooth and stretchy. Add drops of water if it's too dry, or a sprinkle of flour if it's sticky.*

3. *Now start sculpting!*

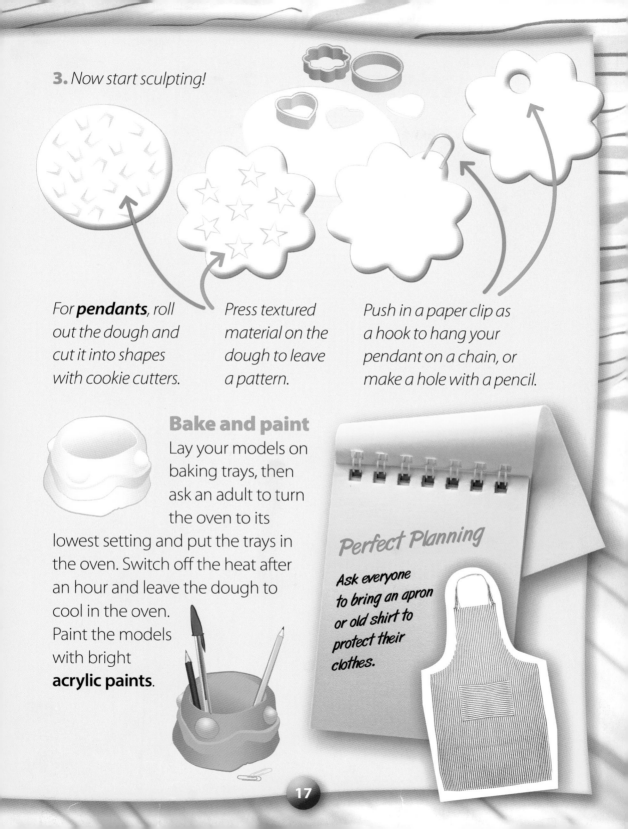

For **pendants**, roll out the dough and cut it into shapes with cookie cutters.

Press textured material on the dough to leave a pattern.

Push in a paper clip as a hook to hang your pendant on a chain, or make a hole with a pencil.

Bake and paint

Lay your models on baking trays, then ask an adult to turn the oven to its lowest setting and put the trays in the oven. Switch off the heat after an hour and leave the dough to cool in the oven. Paint the models with bright **acrylic paints**.

Perfect Planning

Ask everyone to bring an apron or old shirt to protect their clothes.

17

Amazing origami

Try origami, the Japanese art of paper folding. You can buy special origami paper, but squares of ordinary paper or gift wrap work just as well.

Sweethearts

These hearts only take a minute to make. Experiment with sizes and colors, then write secret messages under the flaps!

1. *Fold a square of gift wrap or colored paper in half, corner to corner, then in half the other way, like this. Unfold.*

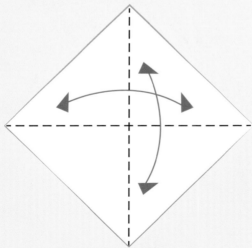

Press firmly along folds to make sharp creases.

2. *Fold the top point into the center, using the creases as guides.*

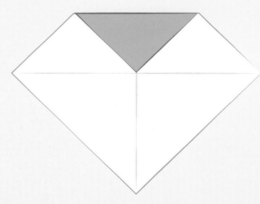

3. *Fold the bottom point up to the top.*

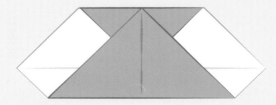

4. Fold each side into the middle, lining up the edge with the center crease.

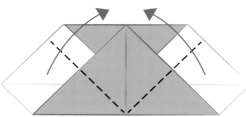

5. Turn over the heart. Carefully fold in the side and top points.

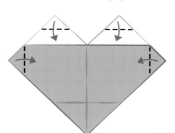

6. Turn it over again and you're done!

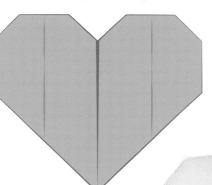

Perfect Planning

Origami needs a flat surface, so clear a space on a desk or table, or hand out big books to rest on.

Clever cards

Making your own greetings cards is lots of fun. Give everyone a piece of thick card, then cut out photos from magazines to create collages, or paper shapes to make mosaic patterns.

Fab flowers

These easy 3D flower cards look really effective.

1. *Cut a 5 inch (12 cm) x 4 inch (10 cm) rectangle of colored card and fold it in half.*

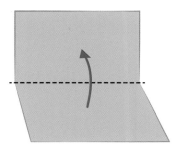

2. *Fold it in half again.*

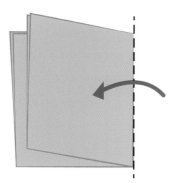

3. *Fold up the top layer to make a triangle, like this.*

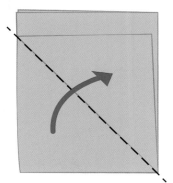

4. *Turn over the paper and do the same on the other side.*

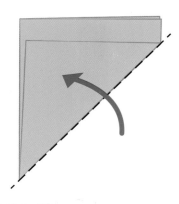

5. Draw a curved line across the triangle to make a petal shape. Cut along it, through all the layers of paper.

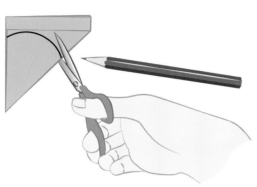

6. Open up the flower shape.

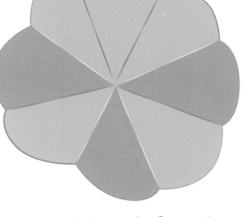

7. Cut more flowers in different colors, or try using gift wrap, tissue paper, or **cellophane**. Make smaller flowers by drawing the curve in step 5 lower, and change the petal shape by making your curve wavy.

8. Layer the flower shapes and glue them together on your card. Stick a button, bead, or plastic gem in the middle of each.

Perfect Planning

See if you have any saw-edged scissors called pinking shears—they create cool zigzag edges.

Glossary

acrylic paints

Colorful, fast-drying paints that can be mixed with water or used straight from the tube. They don't wash off when dry, so don't get them on clothes!

cellophane

A thin, crinkly, see-through material that comes in different colors for craft projects.

felt

Fabric made from matted, pressed wool. Felt is cheap to buy and comes in lots of different colors.

fray

To unravel into loose threads at the edges.

knead

To fold and press dough with your hands until it feels smooth and stretchy.

loom

A frame used for weaving. It holds one set of threads in place lengthwise, while other threads are passed under and over from side to side.

macramé

The art of tying knots to make patterns. As well as bracelets and necklaces, macramé is often used to make wall hangings, bedspreads, and hammocks.

masking tape

White sticky tape that is easy to tear into strips and peel off again.

mosaic

A design made up of lots of small pieces of paper or other materials.

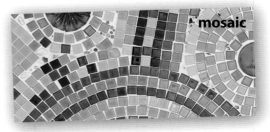
mosaic

origami

A Japanese way of folding paper to create models without any cutting or sticking.

pendant

A piece of jewelry that hangs from a chain or cord.

salt dough

A simple modeling dough made with flour and salt. It sets hard when heated and is easy to paint.

spool

A cylinder, usually made of wood, plastic, or cardboard.

weaving

Lacing together two sets of threads, one set going lengthwise and the other across it.

spools

Web sites

en.origami-club.com

Find instructions for making just about any origami model you can imagine.

www.free-macrame-patterns.com/macrame-for-kids.html

Follow step-by-step instructions to make macramé bracelets, key rings, bags, belts, and decorations.

lifestyle.howstuffworks.com/crafts/bead-crafts

Look at lots of inventive craft projects using beads.

Index